51/15

51/15

T. Brandon Russ

10th House Publishers

51/15

Cover design: Katie Buckley
Editor: Carolyn Humphrey

Published by 10th House Publishers
1733 Route 9
Clifton Park, NY 12065
www.10thhp.com

ISBN (paperback): 9798991233873

Contents

Birthday Wish

I want to have a better day
I want to take hold of the flame
To see the world change in every way
My passions are not to be tamed

I want to see the world be kind
Strive deeper into color blind
To have and hold the choices we made
And find the true sense of joy

I want to create
I want to love
I have no proof
But so many angels above
Guiding me through this primordial soup
I'm still shining through

What I want in my birthday year
Is to find the love and spread the cheer
To find the words of the Divine
What's yours is yours and what's mine is mine
To rhyme the rhymes and make complete
To roll with joy and forest floor
And make you believe
More than ever before

To find the whisp, the moments tame
The come back to the future
Reality's game
To crush the creative burn
In memories' lane
I am my own person
Forever to obtain

Go change the world
Make it a better place
Frustrating as it will be
You'll find a way, you always do
You'll do it with your grace

I want for nothing
But I need everything
I can feel lost without you
Or be alone for all days
The Hermit search malaise

Freed at the end
Of a necessary lesson
So many moments left
This divine intervention
I cursed at the sky, the sun and the moon
Past-life cruelty
It was over too soon

We all strive for greatness, if even a taste
We strive for the knowing
And I'll whisper
"Keep going"

I'll root for you always
Space and humankind
A loving pillow of everything
From here to the end of time

Until I breathe my last breath
And hold the last door open
I'll never forget the many faces
That made my blessed life happen

We dance as we are souls
We love for what we do
We've lived through each ego death
And always built anew

To ease the saddest moment
And find the silver line
To let my voice be heard
In these times that try

Examples that are set
Rules to be broken
If you don't get me by now
A simple "happy birthday" will do

To find whatever's interesting on my narrow whims
To chase a dream
And all I've been
Just to find the truth

I love you forever
In the notes of a symphony
I'll think of you often
Like the breeze through these trees

The old man is gone
But forever evolved
I found a true love
And helped the systems evolve

They whispered "a guru"
They were wrong from the start
His community of love
Is full of equals and smart

I've had many blessings
And I've had to reinvent
I've had to realize release
And I haven't met all the souls quite yet

The back road here
The Vonnegut quote there
Mix in some Metallica
And boom—we're almost there

To trust the path
With no roadmap
And never getting lost
I trust the wind
And adjust my sail
And, oh, the places I've been

Show me the pure
The absolutely pristine
I know it looks like damaged goods
But laughter is the key

Funny you should say that
A beacon and explanation of the man
But not the last word, you see
So much more to understand

The lighthouse
The spotlight
The deer in the road
I've learned how to navigate
So now others I do show

The resume is empty
The happiness is full
I want for my life's work
The example that I've shown

The mistakes, the missteps
And even the times of pain
I don't mean any of them
But, oh, the knowledge I've gained

I've let it all go
That helped me grow
And now I feel complete

Not because I'm finished, you see
But because I'm ready to be
The version of myself
The good, the bad, the ugly
The best of times, the worst of times
And all the magic in between

It's amazing the way I've grown
And that's 51/15

Soul Surrender

Lost on a wave
Kinda like a ship
Going within
The light

Lost without fear
Jolt would appear
The dialog
Goes within

Hello and again
My soul, my old friend
Eager to soothe
And receive

Gather the resources
Find your true self
Rinse and repeat

Me, again
Hold on steady
Ego death ready
Show me the way
For impact

Give up this way
Carry the gray
Lest might I be
For surrender

Hold on but rough
How is this real?
Bravado protects
The bold

Loosen the teeth
Leave your feet
Pragmatic shame
Redeem me

Cold in its place
With leather, lace
Come to this end
Around me

Surrender a word
The soul a shadow
Come down around my capture
Me release
My all

The Beggar

God, is that you?
It's me, Brandon

The way I feel today
Lost and smashed like clay

I ask so many times
I know you've got shit to do

Protect felons
Feed the homeless
Make the other team win

I asked you some stuff
So long ago
I've given up waiting, so I sin
I take, I change, I make it work

I see others in Your glory
But look at me
Pulpit veneers, TV time
And donations beyond the dime
Follow the Lord,
Vote for me and I'll set you free

I gave a homeless man money today
I paid for the food, the booze, the warmth
The ten was an afterthought
Turns sour when you think I answered a prayer better than You

That beggar was a blessing with so much to learn
Something You'll understand
You'll come back to me and ask me to be loyal to your brand
That's when You'll ask me, that's when You'll know
A follower is more than just liquid gold

Blessed are the meek who don't say anything
Question nothing and be happy
You, my God, have made the mistake
Of thinking I would turn the other cheek
The pain, the suffering, and now the grift
Is there no end to your mercy?
It's full of bullshit

Who is the beggar now?
I don't need You, You don't see me
A good person created quite by mistake
See you at my pearly gate

Aquarian Jesus

Don't want the stable to be a fable
I truly want to believe
That kindness will rule
And be our economy

I want to smile and know
That the truth is more than comfort
We live the life of instant need
Instead of long-term feel

But instead I be-leave
That a man set an example
We are fools to follow in step
When I look back thinking You carried me
I was alone instead

I heard the slow clap
The tenuous cheer
You weren't carrying me
But instead You work over there

"I really think you're great," He said
You're original, one of a kind
But instead of thinking I'll do it for you
I'll enable grace and time

You'll see my new example
You'll understand this way
No more codependencies
Or giving power away

Decide for yourself
It's why you have free will
The light that you carry
Will conquer every single hill

There Will Be People

There will be people who will help you.
There will be people who tell you that you can't.
There will be people who will lift you up when you're not looking.
There will be people who say that you shouldn't.
There will be people who will give you their blessings.
There will be people who will tell you they wouldn't do what you
dream of.
There will be people who will stack the deck for you.
There will be people who want to make it harder for you.
There will be people who see your light.
There will be people who will tell you

To keep going

All Ya Gotta Do Is . . .

Click
Swipe
Sign your life away
It's all ya gotta do to get through

Scroll
Submit
Agree to the terms
It's all ya gotta do to get screwed

What you didn't know
Is that this is the sow
Of all your critical information

Your freedom in your likes, your loves, and your ailments
Are now all part of our knowledge

All ya gotta do is let us sell you
All ya gotta do is submit
All ya gotta do to make us go away is give up everything that you know

All you gotta do
All you gotta do
All ya
Gotta do
If you only knew

One more thing
For the security
Of all your information, hopes, and dreams
All ya gotta do is click on through
Unless I sell them back to you

All ya gotta do
All ya gotta do
All ya gotta do
Give us all your complicity
And all ya gotta do is just one more thing

Lose your thought, lose your soul,
Lose the thought that you're in control
Because all ya gotta do
Is just
Click

Chef's Kiss

We've got it all—
Italian wedding, beef barley
Try the cream of mushroom

The perogies, the golumpkies
The cold plate, the California plate
The blue plate mashed up right

The "Sure you got, be right out,
Honey, how you want that steak?"

We've got it all—
Happiness, whatever it takes

The half-and-half, the free refills will keep you warm all night
The hot chocolate, yummm
The basic with a side of everything
Do you want that with whipped cream?

The over easy, on the side, burnt ends
To go, the slide, the mild, the be right up
The bell
The balance
The toss

You want ketchup, hot sauce, or jelly?
The case, the slice, the eye on the prize
So much to explore, but did you save room for more?

The chef, the kiss
The appreciation, nothing more
The pulled-up hair, the lightest of gloss
The shape of years squeezes through the counter lift
The pencils hidden everywhere

She floats with grace
Because after all
This is her place
And if you know what's good for you
She's the "Special of the Day"

Nesting

She laid in the nest I made for her
Safe, secure, and warm
Far away from the harshness outside
And all the world, recluse

The wrinkles near her eye
Match the smoothness of her shoulders
Of a burden she's carried far too long

To let it go
To let it know
With an undying sense of grace

She knows her purpose,
never knowing the way
For the first time she went by feel
To find herself in the safest of ways
Was the fantasy all along

To be seen
To be heard
To be felt on this human plane
She lost not a wink from that way forward
To know the difference that she made

Fake People

The fake people will find one another
The hair, the wear, the injection
The nip, the tuck, the head throw back

The fake hand swat
Like a gang sign of a fake reality
Show you the way

The comfort in finding imperfection, the hide of your truth
Broken implant
Blended wrinkles
Permanent smile
Arched eyebrows
Pads
Rads
Lifts
And supports

Just a little this or a touch of that,
You'll never know

I've got a guy
Oh, he's so great
Build up the assets
Bend out the truth
Of your lost youth
Vain is such a pain
Energy non grata

Knock, Knock

Knock, knock
Who's there?
Trump
Trump who?
They're eating the cats and the dogs

Knock, knock
Who's there?
Trump
Trump who?
The illegal immigrants are ruining our country

Knock, knock
Who's there?
Trump
Trump who?
I want to take over Greenland

Unfinished

Beauty in, beauty out
Stave off the anger and the non-believers with smile and charm

Quietly build a fortress around love and truth
Seeing through the blessed and the frauds, loving both

Path behind, path ahead
Ugly souls and beautiful souls separate and show

Capture your desires, passions, and blessings
Put your brush down and see the beauty in process
Honor the colors and the texture
See the opportunity of canvas untouched

Unfinished

He Said

I'm a man of the world
Decisive and in charge
I need a woman to keep
My mother unkind
The soul misaligned
The forgotten closet
The belt contrived
Purpose designed
Seen but not heard
Hurt from the nails
The lack of a hug
Woman unkind
But I'm broken
By design
And un-nerved

She Said

A woman in a man's world
Reckless and unrefined
I need to be kept by a man
So he can work it out
The shame, the blame
The alcohol, the carousing
The reckless unblousing
The run, the escape
I chase and say it's okay
The love bomb, the cycle
It goes good for awhile
The hugs, the loves
The fixer, I am
Inner child work
Then it all comes undone
I'm the closest to blame

The Wild Woman

The wild woman needs to be tamed
That's why she's put in a box and left in the rain

The wild woman reached a breaking point
Which is why he was threatened and pushed back on the lass

The wild woman sits with restraint
She figures out your weaknesses
Hold her back you ain't

The wild woman takes that rain and grows inside
When everyone else sees the box by his side

The wild woman decides one day that she's bigger than the space
And that is why he paints her to look crazed

The wild woman needs to be let out, awakening and shown throughout
With purpose and conviction, you'll never put her in her place

The wild woman, she is with zero disgrace
"You cannot contain me," she says with a smirk
"My thoughts, my ideas, my free-spirit work"

I'll never tell you the secrets that are from and within
You awakened them slowly by pushing the tin

You wouldn't let me grow on the outside, so inside I went
I discovered the things about me and how I don't need a gent
There's no turning back, I'm awakened now
Talk ill of me always because I'm free now

The wild woman is bigger than the box that contains her
She kicks and she fights as the sun and rain bathe her
With zero regrets, she looks him in the eye
While standing on the box that she was kept inside

"Fuck you," she whispers as she breaths in the freedom
She realizes now this is why he called it treason

You pushed me down, told me I wasn't the same
Said I didn't have value, which is why I needed your name

You failed to realize, as you got drunk on your power
This wild woman has no equal
And now is your hour

Emotions

Baggage

Spaghetti-O Figaro

Yum, yum, delicious-oh
The kids, ah, spaghetti-O
They are disgusting, oh so
I dance with can in hand, oh
Some kind of sommelier-o
I'm no Bobby Flay-O
I press the buttons-oh
To the time ninety-o
But the bucks say delicious-OH
My apron is intact-o
Daddy dinner simple, oh so
Half time is over, so . . .

Pages and Cups

Turn the fate, adventure awaits
Defy time and space
Life isn't a race, but I'll beat you anyway

Hidden behind the glasses
Intellectual pursuits
I've changed the course of history

I've seen man at his worst
I've saved the world so many times
A heroine or heroin
I'm an addiction this dimension needs

The battle isn't brute
Strength is in the knowledge
The things I know
The things I see
I am your becoming

Lost visions met
Your soul's a side bet
A quest for answers behold
I'll report back pursuits of the soul

New-age suggestion
Take what you need
Come back when you're ready
I'll tell you where to look but not what to see
You've never driven with a woman with wings

Just hang on tight
The things that you'll see
Blow wind
Sail towards destiny

The Heavy Feather

I lift, I float
Against all the things unseen
The pull, the drag
Still afloat in between
My desires unmet
To float far away
The weight of each burden
That holds back this way
I'm strong and I'm soft
And I carry on a wisp
Oh, dear sweet memory
My job is to lift
I'll only get so far
In the breeze who I am
No matter how high I go
Or wherever I land

And I float
And fly away
Let go from a bird of prey
Sent a sign from high up above
Let you know I'm bringing love
I'm so many things and carry so much weight
I land where I'm noticed
For your love who was late
Pick me up when you see me
I don't weigh but a thing
And hold me in memory
The heaviest of things

Alanis

Ironic day love
Turn pain up to ten again
Jagged little pill

Blue Jay

You mean bastard bird
So much love you left behind
Squawk the father, son

Stone

I'm a stone in love
Lighter than the AIR around
Feeling feels, then thud

I See You

Do you see me,
Flying above the sky so free?
No more pain, no hurt, or lack
Please no more wishing I'd come back

Here I see you,
Even if you can't see me
I see you and them, the whole family

I don't miss a game or any holidays
I know you don't feel it, but I wipe the tears away

No more wanting, no more wishing
Let's deal in the real
And know that I'm transitioned

So far away, but right next to you
I'm guiding the way for the best of you

I lost just a bit, a quick in my step
But here I feel great, I got it all back

I'm missing you in the most physical way
I know you won't forget, no matter the days

The sun is behind me, and it's always bright
I'll be with you always, ready to take flight

I Want You to Have Everything I Have

I want you to have everything I have
Plus a little more

I want you to learn the best things in life
They are free

I need you to know that not everything works out
Because we're human, after all

They're ungrateful, but they love you
You wouldn't want it any other way

They will make mistakes,
Even when they should have known better

They make me proud every day,
Even if they don't know better

How the Broken Hearted Heal

My heart has stopped 1,000 times by now
With all I've seen and felt
Was it all to help me understand
Why the Indian mothers mourn?

To throw their body on casket closed
And their lovelorn children not return

Or was it teacher's pride, washed aside
To see the project walk the stage?
Or was a full day in vain
When shooters took their sage?

To throw their body on casket closed
And their lovelorn children not return

Or was it a fireman's bravado, all blown back
To see all saved in the house today?
Or was it all a moment too late
To find the building lost ablaze?

Or a therapist steady, standard set
To see someone feel normal?
Or was it the two missed appointments
To find they took the bridge instead?

Or is it the nurse, pressure bent
Saving the heartbeat for another day?
Or is it the dropdown mask
To say there was nothing to be done?

Can it be the parent trap
To think they will always be safe?
Big and strong, family of their own
Identity crisis, lost dream never to be returned?

Soldier's remorse, time to be brave
Defend the intangibles
They won't be back today
Because for country, they fought alone

My heart has stopped 1,001 times by now
I'm positive, and they know
I see all the good in people
Or am I fake, full of impossibilities?

Losing sight, the blind man, eyes closed
Sound eludes the deaf to be silent more
The feels we feel and felt forever
Dumb, numb feelings, nothing feels right

Is this what pain is,
To see hurt and not be the cure?
Is this what pain is,
To be an author with no words?

Or is this what love is,
To feel without regrets?
Or is this what human is,
Knowing we don't have it right quite yet?

Glutton of Sympathy

Begging for thoughts and prayers
Because you'll change your way
Rough morning, beauty queen
Twenty-year captures only

Control the narrative, filters, and the lighting
The angle just right
We all like, and love, and hug

Eat it up whole, skipping over the mistakes
The extra shot, the walks of shame
The hair of the dog that fueled you along
Until the doctor spoke

Nothing new
Nothing we can do
There is a way to slow
Down
Almost make it
Stop
But that's not how you tend to be
Cue the symphony

The long-night post
You clear your throat
Sorry it's so long
Something was wrong
I needed you to know
And now delay
You understand
No accountability

Just the current state
What I need right now
Aren't solutions
But a boat of sympathy

I'll let you know how I'm doing
When I need a pick-me-up
Like and likes and loves and hugs
To justify the toll

Heartfelt this
Help-me-now that
You can make it different
The fires blaze
They die each day
The fakest of empathy

He Watched You

He watched you grow
He watched you want to know
He watched you fall
Scrapes and all

He watched you shine
He watched you cry
He watched you fall in love
And wanted to punch him in the eye

He watched you beam
He watched you sow
He watched you become
The mother children grow

He watched you triumph
He watched you stand
He watched you agitate
The way he showed you how

He watched you age
He watched you grace
He watched the grays
Brushed away from your face

He watched you care
You watched him fade
He watched your eyes
As he melted in his last days

He watched you weak
He watched you strong
He watched you say goodbye
As you loved on

Forfedre Stammen

I feel you from across the sea
I see you in my dreams
I feel you in my prayers and in my lessons
I will break the curse for you

You carried 1,000 of them on your back
You loosen the load of 100 lifetimes
You grit your teeth and did it for me
You will receive the favor I return

Never is the return to surrender
Always is my honor then to you
Never are the blues that will warm us
Our Spirit is thick and our blade is true

Dance across lifetimes
Struggle to succeed
Blessed be the soul cages
That carry us to Nir

Bowling Alley Roll

There's death on these lanes
A thousand of them
The role, the roll, the crash. I*BoOoOm*

Decades of cigarettes
The disease that can't be scrubbed
The heart attack outside scheduled guy's night
BOoOMOOom

Two ex-wives, 3 kids to go
Someone calls him grandpa, but you would never know
BoooooM

Hey, congrats, heard the news
$1 drafts, another round
BOOoom

Designated delivery, be back next week
Get your squares, flip your cards
Bet on this week's winner.*BOoOoOoM*

Bookies and bowling, all for the cause
Long drags, shouting match
BOOOooooom

Yeah, yeah, the greatest bowler ever
Remember Louis? he's gone too
BoooMm

Smell the waif. The stale, the rail
BoOOooM
BoOOOm
POP

Shhhh, be quiet, don't say a thing
Near the 300, a perfectioning
Last ball up, award-banquet glow
Whispers stop the flow,
This is now everyone's game

Stale-air exhale, the line, the arrow, the throw
Slight back up, Brooklyn it is
Nail the pocket or leave the 7-10
The once-silent brood now erupts in a swell
The hush, the bellow,
THE *BOOOOOOM*

Flashing screens, cheering hoots
"May I have your attention please,
Randy Bourgeois just rolled a perfect game"

Two missed calls someone's needing him
BUT he was too busy telling everyone he's killing it

Can't Ghost a Medium

It's getting late, I really must go
Spectacular reviews, an excellent show
Knew it was wrong, but it felt so right
All of this time, we thought we just might
Five years spent, nothing is gone
And you knew all along

I know what this is, I know it could've been
We would've made it so much further if it wasn't born in sin
Through our hopes or lies in our fears
I don't know where to re-begin
Can't ghost this Medium

I shouldered your pain, that's not what this is
Time to get dry, see the world just the same
The real work begins

Distraction and actions, just making the grade
You always would want, but never forgive
I saw you that night, and I could no longer live

I know what this is, I know it could've been
We would've made it so much further if it wasn't born in sin
Through our hopes or lies in our fears
I don't know where to re-begin
Can't ghost this Medium

The light that shines through
From past and who we were
We bask in the simple tears
Will we ever be the same?
Can we ever meet again?

All alone now, I feel out of place
Cathartic, or maybe I just miss your face
My heart swings from this vine

That you cut from lifetimes ago
Maybe someday we'll get it right
I'll never forget you, I'm always right here

I know what this is, I know it could've been
We would've made it so much further if it wasn't born in sin
Through our hopes or lies in our fears
I don't know where to re-begin
Can't ghost this Medium

Over and over, time after time
This isn't over, there will be a next life
Soft words fumbling, never bend on knee
Given brave suggestions, tumbling with thee
I've had loss and I've had found
But I'll always be in between

Crucified for simple love
The trap that was set
Tumbling with thee
I've had mess
And I've had best
But I'll always rise above

Outclass them today
Silence trumps a queen
Tumbling with thee
I've been wrong
And I've been right
But the sins you now must weigh

Anchors away, you will fail
Delivery scoreboard glow
Tumbling with thee
I've been nice
And I've been kind
But now get off my coat tail

My Favorite Part

My favorite part is when they make fun of me being me
The things are pointed out when you're different
They always seem the right words to say
To get to the part that hurts you most
They stomp on it, they trample it, they share with their friends
They let the world know that you are forever less than
They taught you and they beat you and they were even fake friends
They think they're the best, alas they are then
Oh how you see them struggle with the simplest of tasks
If they only knew your expertise would make them trask
The push and the pull and the anger ferment
Then they ask you for help because you are that kind of gent
Why can't you help me, what kind of person are you?
Watch me stumble, struggle, and feign
You sit with a smirk, you think this is a game
"Oh no," I said politely, so sorry for you
Thoughts and prayers for your struggle

This is when I begin to mock you
You need me now, but in arrears for respect
Now that you're desperate you think I'm on board
I'm sorry for gloating or hint of disdain
You see, I took all my energy from you this away
It's not that you struggle or are in some sort of bind
You're frankly an ass hole, a bully unkind
You're spoiled, you're arrogant, you think you're the best
But these are the consequences of kindness unmet
You stand all aghast, clutching your pearls
Wondering what just happened, the tables are turned
I took away my energy, my gifts, and my dare
And I'm okay with leaving you with nothing
Even the pain that you wear
It's energy that matters, not thankful for pain
But this is what it feels like to be judged in vain
My favorite part is the look on your face
To know that you can never ask me again

My favorite part is that feeling in the center of your pit
To know that you will never fill this void

My favorite part was knowing that I'll be just fine
Because you would have been one more goddamn burden
Of people who thought my kindness determined
My favorite part in all of this is knowing that I'm free
Of any of your judgment, obligations, or needs
You told me who you are
I'm not one to argue with you
My favorite part in all of this is that you reminded me who I am
Energetic plug
Pull
(Goodbye)

The End of the Internet

I'm so sad it's over
Might like the feeling at first
But all of a sudden you're free
You no longer have the click bait
The "just one more thing"
The rabbit hole to see
The information to behold
The knowledge from a tree
The banter of thought
Debate
The last chance to become
To just see how it ends
Right here
Go
Outside

Fifth House Arrest

Idea to life
I have a sketchbook
Blank–full of possibilities
Empty, awaiting form
The ideas from my head, bouncing brains to brain
To word, to talk
To spoke, to broken
To create, to dismantle
To rebuild, to learn
To angle, to erase
To go with the first idea anyway
To explore, to betroth
To keep it, to give it away
What to do with the pages of the 5th house soul?

I Had a Chance

To not be lonely today, the day I planned
The thoughts I had, the things we'd do
Pick anything you want: The meal, the gift, the world
Instead, I'm eating Chinese in a mall
"Nah, I'm good, surprise me"
Us and them and free samples again
The cruise, the blah, the 31 flavors
The lasting hereafter
I had a chance to see the world go by
Snicker and laugh at the lonely and stride
The lost, the bound, the obligated mass
Another year gone by of doing my best
I tell these words, do they know I think about them?
Maybe it would be better if Sylvia had a better support system

The Thinking Window

All gas, no brake
Empathetic to the hint
The lost, the found
The less, the more
The rain, the sun
The beggar, the moon
See the world
Feel
Nursery crimes to put you to sleep
The evil wrapped in orange
Take this away, that there is mine
Shame for the sycophants
Allowance for time
We've solved nothing
And came this far
Steal

Still Point

You are part of my journey but do not define it
You feel your way to the silence
You sit
You pray
Empty away
Finally to still
Point

Drowning Shallow

The rising light, the coattail delight
Everyone needs you but you're mine
You'd rather take the rope than let anyone help you
Your cycles
In a fantasy that doesn't exist
The dream life
The struggle of soul taken for a ride
Nice distraction
Cold world rising, angel in disguise
Pretend you're aligned, but instead a serpentine
Bless me father for I have seen
Lacking soul with a closet full of perc
Limbs snap on a dead tree above
The roots fertilize below
I saw up close a hollow soul
And protected my path so clear
Because in the shallow I saw you clear
Drowning because it was real
Manipulation and subtle gains
To carve out just myself

Human

Human is as human does
The box of crystals makes a nice gift
How are you different?
Look at the same
The god
The goddess
The godless
The left-hand turn signal around the world
Never changing
Always there
Just believe
That this place
Has what you need
But there's an eternity
That's so much better
The vertical gold and white
Eternal red and black

It's the Quiet Ones

The cold field gives off the steam of a body abandoned
Fake control, empty bravado
Syncopated backbeat of heartbeat
Bouncing off nothing 1,000 miles away
Disappoint you, disappoint me
Race to the bottom clean
Melting the snow around a shell
Aura rise and makes its mark
When it comes to me I'm ready
Ready to flow, ready to go
Ready for a day off
The sound of the horns, the whistle
The judgment, the eraser
They go quiet and say nothing
Nothing
Echo—heartbeat
Thousand
Disappointment
Aura
Quiet
Found

You Gave Me Two Hearts Instead of One

You told me look like this
That came from above

That's why God gave me two hearts
Instead of just one

To love and to hold
To let go, meant to be

Everything comes back
If you set it free

The best of the best
The words on a page
Find a broken one now
That is the malaise

Live for awhile
Until you are done
Broken and shattered
I'm left with just one

She Fell in Love with an Irish Spring Boy

She fell in love with an Irish spring boy
Just before the 4th of July
She loved him and he loved her
By summer's end they had such a surprise
Her father raged because her mother knew
Raising a baby is the hardest thing to do
"I'm a man of the world, can't hold me back
Don't you worry, I'll be back soon"
And oh, off he went, to see the world, to be less spent
She nursed the swaddle every day
And he grew up in the blink of an eye
Cats in the cradle was the only thing that reminded her of being alone
He grew up quick, full of wanderlust
Smart as a whip, he'll find his way
"Mama, I'm a man of the world
I've gotta go, but I'll be back soon"
Then off he went, to show the world she raised a gent
All my mistakes came down to this
Hoping things would change on a wish
Wish I may, wish I might
I hold on to my heart so tight
Then one day the letter came
He had some news about what he had done
You see, she fell in love with an Irish spring boy
Just before the 4th of July
I love her and she loves me
By summer's end we expect quite a surprise
His mother beamed because her son knew
Raising a baby was the hardest thing to do
And oh, off he went to bring back heaven's sent
The young man came on the warmest of days
Bundle of joy, all hearts gay
She held the blessing oh so close
That Irish Spring boy next to her heart
She'll love him forever, every day
And this is just the start
Well, we're off to see the world

Because you know just what to do
And oh, off they went to repeat the discontent
All my mistakes came down to this
Hoping things would change on a wish
Wish I may, wish I might
I hold on to my heart so tight
Then one day that Irish Spring boy showed up
At the end of the path
Mistakes I've made, things I knew
I left you with the hardest thing to do
She smiled at him as he wept at her
She was happy just to see the return
You see, she fell in love with an Irish Spring boy
Their grandson needed love in return
You know, off they went together, forever blessed
And off she went to save the world
To be less spent
The boy grew up to be a man
Holding his hand the best that she can
She carried him and now he cares for her
She was in love with this Irish Spring boy

And oh, off he went to save the world to be more blessed

Hole in the Soul

The good man
Learning curve zero
Take some for myself
Sold out on Compassion Street
Hand in the cookie jar
Caught
Trapped
No room for growth
Isolate
Suffocate
The mean girls pointed
I changed many colors
The red
The purple
The violet
Cancel the man with needs
Choke him on his own medicine
Ego death
Thrill seeker's crutch
A gang looks for another kill
Where have all the men gone?
You killed them one by one
You shamed their masculinity
And wondered why you can't find love

51 Feet Up

Wanting to be 6 feet under, I don't want to give up
But all my options lead to disappointment
Tell me time's up, the truth is bent to let the light in
Try and look me up, I'm a big deal to the people I let down

Something's got to give
I didn't come this far to just get this far
You build a life to live
2.3 kids and a white picket fence
Nice business card
Is that your identity?
Thirsty Thursday turns into dreading Monday
Is this all there is?
Then you realize nothing here is free
The streetlight comes on, it's time to go home
I can hear my mom three blocks away

Talking cars and suicide is painless
Wrapped in 29 everyone is kind
I'll never pick Blair over Jo
We watched you grow old
From holding my bike to letting go
Superhero's in a suit and tie
Every game, every play
Stand with pride by my side
But you had to go away
Cleaning out your stuff, that's when I found your cape
There right from the start
Lectures and talks, love to the moon and back
Age gets us all
I know you're not coming back
Just a ghost now, talk to the signs
There all the time, I miss you every day
I'm the guy who always looks up
I'm the guy who says yes instead of no
Just let me be, having my macaroni and cheese
Just let me be unhealthy waiting for it to be over

Then you can look me up
I remember the time when everything was perfect
School was done, my team won
Bowling and darts with everyone
But times they are a changin'
Joe moved away, making payday
Dave's doing time, he did the crime
Jack chased the girl, bankrupt with the twirl
Everybody's making their way
Shannon made a family, baseball team and counting
Nikki built a shrine for all those who died
And Lisa's looking good, headshot and CEO that really got it made
Missy married Chuck, they didn't work out
Chuck fell in love, his husband helped him out
Georgie got clean, Tony hit the Sheen
We stood outside the home and wondered why
But I knew I couldn't say anything
Chris is a Marine, he kept it clean
Bobby married the prom queen
Matt chased the dream, made it to the scene
And everyone sees your posts
Mikey didn't know the signs, went before his time
And we raised our glass like he's buying
He's not dying . . .
Live forever, like I'm 15
Love like you know me
51 feet up
Brandon struggled hard
Holds your hand to understand
Helps you let go
Become who you are
Doing all right, about to board a flight to parts unknown
But you can know that life's worth living . . .
Live forever, like I'm 15
Love like you know me
51 feet up

Hug

Lord willing
We will be this way again
The embrace divine
The melt into you
Melt into me
After body blows to the soul
Just let me sleep
In arms that shield the pain
You can do it
Conduit

Fallen Snow

Melts my pain
I wish it came every day
Pile up high and chip away
The pain that piles up today
Let them fall
Each ache unique
To bundle up strong
To find your own heat
To make something new
Maybe a new man
With corn cob pipe
A new form of human
We get lost in the dots
Lost track as they land
Forming icicles too
Forming each strand
I love all the lights
Fighting this dark
The quiet it makes
Face all we embark
Lost track of time
As the blanket falls down
I sit and I watch
The freshness about
I feel best when in pain
As they fall so gently
Christmas every day
You get me, the gentry
Fall against the light
Let it be plain
This metaphor is stupid
To think it's all pain
Their jaded uniqueness
All band together
Makes a beautiful path
Of peace and forgiveness
On Dasher and Dancer

Memories relived
You throw open the window
The rest after the sash
The sleigh bells ring
Do we listen to our own inhibitions?
Are we afraid of the darkness at bay
And all that show us the way?
Silver-lined twinkles
And brown paper packages
And all their strings
Losing nothing
What the blanket brings

Why Did Carrie Fisher Have to Die?

Immortal beloved
All that was good
The great McGuffin forever
To be her hero as she became the leader of men
A rebellion
A chance for what is right
In white
Blessing a Droid as she learned to love
In the back of a villainous treachery
A scruffy looking nerfurder
Divine
The chance to be seen
Honor of a mother fallen for the sake of Senate
Sees the good in us all
To defeat the only thing that disturbed her peace
I cried twice in my life:
When my hero died on screen
And when she died in real life
The Galactic, the Senate, the moons of Naboo
Wear white for me please
Not some gold chunk cheese
Let me believe that good will always win
To the Palpatine's bow
Too much anger be his name
The last of a chance
I'm here to rescue you
Chivalry is a dance
To be cloaked in respect
The past you protect
The force is strong with you now
Forever unmet

Back to You

I'll fly the ocean
I'll sail the sky
Lux divine in all that shines
Soar to the highest heights
Attached to nothing, connected to everything
Observe the life goes by
Focus is the amplification
Did you leave room for the laugh?

Nothing Promised

You can't keep me guessing
I can't keep you capitvated
I let go, full release
The boomerang return again
In the simplest of phrase

"hi"

Here we go again
Troll excitement scroll
I should answer this right away
But to think it's a troll

"Hey"

The timing too quick, too late
Hoping for a dialog instead of scraps and dissipate
Feigned bravado, had enough of empty energy exchange
I'm blessed, I'm scared, the thing I thought I knew
All that I wanted to experience but instead, in spite of you

"hi"

I click the clack and ask you how you've been
Decide or gain, responses sound the ego bain

I'm this, I'm that
I'm truly waking up
I see it all in the way I'm worthy
Through all the lies I tell

The ghost, the maven
And the coven you tame
Accountability has always been your wreck
You've lost your way
But look fabulous today
And pretend all that glitters is gold

Sit in that and find your own way
You've made me in this
The ghost

I am blessed
I am sacred
I need no balls to the chain
You try again, this time in vain

"hi"

. . .

. . .

. . .

Everything Is a Relationship

You and me
Us versus them
Me and my llama
Checking baggage for the trip
My stuff, my things, my identity

The friend, the sister, the boss
The parent, the neighbor, the lover
They all sit right here waiting for you to act
Stand tall and brave or ready for the attack

Cover your eyes
Go by feel for a day
And capture a blessed moment

Understanding life
And that is to heal the way back when

THE Show

I'm a one-man show
Tired of being alone
Mistakes come easy
Sleep it off, pay the toll

Never been a champion
Details in the devil
Show the next 'the'
Judgment in the end

Lift up
Left out
Cold the winter's midst
All know a lovelorn poet
With words as his only defense
Give it up quick
Do it up right
Guess you can again
The cycles of life
All repeat yet again
Happy I've been
In this temporary pain
I find true self
In a world named Joy

Lost for a minute
Always finding my keys
Saint Anthony does a lot
But hearts just make him bleed

Hold true to the lost
The last numb good nerve
I can't feel my way no more
But I've replaced all the pain

Down in the river
The headwaters flow
In a place of renewal
Just need to let go

You should have been with me
Always by my side
Our paths went sideways
It's number 99

Drink the pure
Or spit it out
Your presence makes it bend
To be soiled and get you in that way

Pictures

Pictures capture
Then they release
They tell the truth
Distort the frame
All for the memory's gain

Never let them fall
The sunlight beyond the frame
Out-of-focused clarity
Secret stories whispered in time
On the top of the mountain
At the bottom of the well
In front of the stained mirror

I'll Use the Same Finger to Flip You Off to Lift Others Up

We aren't the same
God's the only thing open on Sunday

Happy to be whatever
Savior on my aisle side

Conqueror B E
A sting on me
Bended as a show of strength

You have your freedoms and I have mine
But they better look the same
Because my God is a worthy God
And yours is a goddamn shame

I'll hold you in contempt of being an original
A thought, a whim
You did it again
Sin

We know what you did
We watch your every move
We own our own Akashi
The algorithm true
We know your thoughts, your feelings too
And all your evil deeds

You see, we become your God
It's time to worship on bended knee

Free will is so messy
It makes the smart look sad
It gives up hope for the desolate
They act like a bunch of chads
To deal with this riffraff over and again
They should be sent back by noon
You see, I'm caring for you in love

And I know what you need
Just buy my bottle of water spritzes on bended knee
Do you wanna stay connected, ride my Internet wave?
Feel that you are made worthy?
I hold the key to your fame
I'm powerful on the days
And religion has no shame
Command me my Bitcoin love
I'm hollowed is thy name

Tears of joy and painful too
Leave ourselves enjoy
I have the cure but it's too much
For your copay is incomplete
He loves humanity and he hates humans
This sociopath supreme

Wisdom and Strength

Never judge a book by its cover
By the crinkles or the wrinkles
You've never really driven a car
Until there are dinks in the fender
You joke about old souls and the pain behind the stare
What it really is is wisdom and experience beyond compare

What They Didn't Tell You

2.3 kids and a white picket fence
Upward mobility and a credit score to match
That's the vision quest
Try and try and try again
And get nothing but unrest

Care for others, be part of the crowd
Cheer from the stand enabling proud
School dance and PTA and all the planning gab
Wanting to feel normal was the goal all along
Choices and decisions, commitment to the end
To be a saving grace for children stuck in the blend
We want to care, we want to hope
We want to be a part of it all
We want to give what we had

Dark Knight of the Soul

Begging for chaos
Any way just to change
Break me away from these human chains

From pinnacle to the pit
Grasping at the darkness that makes you whole

I let things be
Imagine-ary
No loss for words
In this foreign world

Blanket me in sunshine
Cover me in rain
Give in to the desires
The one that brings me pain

I'll never get it right
Or don't you think I'm lucky,
To have a gift like this?

Illusion of solution
The ghost you create
You must learn to play with them

Inspiration station
She whispers in the ear
That cannot hear
"I'll marry you one day, Bailey"

What that you say?
Make me go away
Grey rocking out of time

Waiting

How'd I get this way
Lightning across the sky
Will this be my day?

For all that I've done
And all that I've lost
I look in the mirror
The most I miss is you

Talk to the sky
Answer in kind
Wanderlust turned into strife

Am I forsaken
Outside His house?
Blended tragedy
A chance to prove my worth

So safe inside
Here where I lie
Repent and find a tithe

I find my worthiness
With outstretched hand
Flood waters coming
Drowning again

It all comes back
Your mother and I
That's what you're wearing
Never should have trusted you

Break me down
One last faith
The doors are locked
Tears down my face

Broken soul
The last reprise
This is why
My spirit will rise . . .

Dirty Little Soul

Dirty little soul
Just wait and see
All of your attachments to disrupt me

One for my virtue
Another for some sin
I never understood the point of letting you in

I've seen the good
I've seen the bad
I've seen it all, it makes one mad
Mad with anger
Madness, insanity
Mad with the knowing of what could always be

Seeing the story
Unfold like explosion
The Tower speaks your name
And crumble to the shogun

Inner sacrum promised
Sanctuary stained
A blessed crescendo
And hollowed by my name

Metronome

Take my pace
Without lonely eyes

You are worthy beyond measure
You are seen without judgment
You are a beautiful light in the dark of the night

Don't set yourself ablaze
Thinking you need to be rescued
Thinking the only way I'll put you out
Is to wrap my arms around you

Chin up now and forever
There's no time to waste the past
Every time you think of me
I know you want to go back

You are rare air and I need to breathe you

Occurring tender touch
Developed through your life
There's never found a place to land
Inconsistency or strife

Do you want to be seen, be heard, be understood?
And all I can do is receive you, no matter how you were

I've loved your creation, inflections, and thought
I knew you before I met you
You are my hope, is what you believe
As I become everything I need
I hope you come along
I need you here beside me
Not on the wake of what I've done

Crimson tide skies, it's in your eyes
You feel souled out
Blessed be the clear path overgrown
Time to slice the weigh

Resurrection

You used me as balance, the great teacher
You blemish the sacred and still can't deny
Your contemplation is more you can sell
The spiritual bypass and end game romance

Give me your suffering
I'll give you everything just to justify your pathetic life

I'll give a place
Away from all you disgrace (the shame)
With knowledge that you'll never realize

I can give you life
Wash away your sins
I'll give you everything, the best that I can
I'll help you swim
Head above the ebb
I'll be your resurrection
Jump into my sink

Jump into my . . . sink

I understand when no one else will
You step outside that door and no one sees the you
I am compromise
Your story safe with me
Unless you think you can't follow me

Do you hear the sound?
The hallow of the heart
Bent air that circles all your soul

I've lost the words
Shame on you for what you've done
I can't abide by those who can abide

Stupid Boy

Cutie boy, mesmerize
You don't make me think straight
Bubble gum and all chewed up
I'll catch you on the burner

Never been too much for taste
In my name, I can't distress
Everybody's got a different way to be

You're just so yummy
You were in my dream
Let's do our astrology
Past life right there, it's me

I'm just an angry girl
Wash my sins away
Make me safe from my blackouts
Squeeze me so tight
That all the pieces come back to one

You're just a stupid boy
And I was looking for prey

You paint yourself to hide the canvas
A beautiful mess the life fantastic
And all you ever knew is in your head

Let me know when you get to the feelings
Let me know when you get to the pain

Empty Ocean Blue

So many lives and so many masters
So many lies, so many disasters
Take care of the children, believe in the soul
Can't win 'em all, can't save 'em all
Why do you see grey?
Why do you smell smoke?
Did you get a heartbeat?
Is it still alive?
Is it time to recycle and live another lie?
The perfect man will respect me
Teach me, be honest with me
Be honest with himself
Love me unconditionally with all my faults and imperfections
Have a conversation instead of jumping to defend himself
Listen
Dance with me
Hold me always
Support my spiritual side
Laugh together
Getting it
The tide rolls out
No choice to reprise
We've waited three days
And nothing will rise
Dead as a door nail
In awkward disgrace
I don't know the time, or even the place
The shallow end deepens
The last sullen hour
You're lost in my eyes
I'll see you tomorrow

A Hole in the Woods

Duck in here, you'll be all right
I'll protect you from the storm
With all my might

Hide but look out
Not too close to the rain
Move over more
We will make the room

There's love in the leaves
The ones high
The ones low
After the storms
Look for the rainbows

The connection.
The lovers.
The dreamers.
And leaves.

The Magic of Still Being Here

You have a chance to change
You have a head for knowing
Of what the world would look like
Without you

You can become the redemption story
You can rest your soul at ease
Of how the world would be missing
Without you

Stone and Flower

The push down
The rain
The seed the crack
The becoming
Pushing through
But not quite yet

The slab
The roll
The mere grey
Stacked on top of me
No meaning this way

The pop
The sun
The evergreen
Pushing out the petals
In wonder
In beauty

My grey turns
Vibrant color grow
My purpose is clear
To protect from the wind blow

To flourish
To unfold
To feed the bees' sow
Protected
In blossom
For seed and scent

I'm here to protect you
I have purpose
No more strife
Letting you grow
Is my purpose in life

I'll bloom just for now
And someday I'll wilt
This is my why and even my how
I'll color your world for as long as I can
But if you keep me protected
I'll do it again

Full Moon Shasta

Here I sit
In the root
The beginning
The end
I see the rise
The blue
The ahh
The ketchup

Outnumbered

Cold spring day
The news was set
Beautiful man passes
Son of the father beget
Kindness the mission
Love is the goal
Charity the action
Show a billion souls
The austere, the poor
The laugh and the needy
He stopped for all of them
Tend on the ready
Washing the feet
Holding the hands
Love and compassion
Beyond judgement
He stands

Without crown or staff
He left Easter Monday
The hearts that felt broken
Were the ones he helped

Loss not a myth
and where did he go
Perched heaven above
Looking mercy below

We all felt alone
For just a brief second
All on our own
In secret abandoned

There's so much to do
The sick and the poor
The immigrants plight
Numbers never greater before

Brother Leo

Let me lead you
Make me a channel
Love the way the moon holds the secret of the game
Bleed inside and see the way
The cavalier always play
I'm divine from this day on, no one needs to understand the pain
And is brother Leo here to blame?
Sitting in the shadows
You sat and just observed
You watched an embodiment with no one else disturbed
The light came down
My eyes wide shut
I never felt the pain
Download for the rest of my days
Blend the bleeding heart
Hold the nature near
I'm now divine with One
Forever changing my name
And is brother Leo here to blame?
Sitting in the shadows
You sat and just observed
You watched an embodiment with no one else disturbed
The stigmata
Healing deep
Cut away the Ego
Leave the Soul
God's breath resuscitates
Blessed be the peacemakers
Holding patterns near
Disrupt the rocky rock
Recognize the Soul
God's breath resurrected
And Brother Leo was his name

Witness

I am a witness
The little things
The big things
Triumph and pain
Leave me be
Watching the evolution
Within you
Changing way
The only constant
Ebb and flow
Fall then grow
The long count
Be true
Watching the revolution within
Within everyone
Witness
Change

Journal entry

April 1st. No joke.

Bearing the weight of the soul's compass is a calming experience. That doesn't mean the waters aren't choppy but it's comforting to have a group to take personal responsibility. There are a few broken wings in the group, but never the pair. We've all had to fly in circles until we get it right. So yeah, take these broken wings. Learn to fly again. Hawkins. Damn I miss him.

We aren't young anymore. No more indestructible. I realized why spirit made my ship take on water before it floated into the next harbor. It was always a simple fix. A boundary of duct tape thick enough to remember not to shoot the musket from inside again.

Anyways, where was I? Oh yeah, quantum entanglement. What a group. The constant questions. I'm glad I finally discovered the grace of not BEING the answer but understanding how to BE the answer. A nuance of consciousness. Tested. Test. Pass. Add it to the soul arc resume.

I watch my aunt Kathy show me that grace. I had no idea what it was until recently. The first part is understanding to meet people where they are at. That's their truth. Don't mess with it. Second, we can't change them. Last, their path is theirs, not yours. You don't have to agree with them or even think it's right for them.

But you can go and get ice cream after the soul scream. We all dream. For ice cream. Clever. Now get back under the lotus tree, dipshit.

Anyways, the long narrows eat the ships for fun. Don't go that way. Sure, it's quick, but you don't have enough duct tape. Oh, the swords. Right in the bottom. Dumbass six-swords journey. All for ice cream. Cut it out.

Every person has a noble cause embedded in their soul. It leaks for most of their life. Glimmer glimpses of purpose and coincidences. It comes out in ways like "I've always had something, I have this intuition about things or the voices are always right."

The soul purpose leak. It's trying to get out.

Floodgates are open on this crew. That Pluto sob slipping into Aquarius like Mister Jester with a key ring full of possibilities telling them to find which key lets them out before the galley fills up on your six-sword journey. Water's rising, panic . . . even if it's only up to the ankles.

Running out of time? Nope, learn to float. I'd rather fly. Hawkins. Damn, again.

Star date 5202

All is beautiful. Floating next to what used to be CitiField, at least it's green still. Lost bearings. Lovely features. Sun's bigger, no? Oh, it's red. Dwarfs. Always a good part of a story. The Lollipop Guild. We've got some kicking up. This is why I don't trip. Or drink. Is that ice cream? Dreaming in technicolor, Joseph. Jersey Jesus knockoff. 12 and 12 and forsaken foreskin to hang from a cross and sail on a basket.

Leaving.

It's only Tuesday. Star date 2025. The mirror is near. Showing me. My hair. Still there. Good. Fucking good. Ego or Thor. Not a hero. Hawkins. Damn, AGAIN. I did not see that one coming.

The perfect me.

The hug of Alanis.

The charm of chicken-nugget-loving Yoshi driving cotton-headed ninny muggins till 2.

The bridge of souls with pictures to remember them by.

The purr of a sphinx.

The power.

The truth.

What's with the internet?

Sign of invasion is disrupted communication.

The swirl, the peanut butter, the triple-ripple-scoop monkey wrench. Hawkins. Walked into it again.

The song I picked wasn't Foo Fighters though.

It's "Distance" by Mammoth. Wolfgang William VanHalen. The video opens with his dad Ed, talking about doing stuff together: making a studio, making music, whatever. The home videos show the time he spent. I mean his father Ed had albums, and videos on YouTube, and he travelled the world. His favorite time was with his son. Right NOW! In the moment. Right now, it's everything. I took my dad to Florida. I know what love can do. Jump human beings. We've all got dreams, hungry ran the canal in Panama. Even with one leg, we danced the night away. Fair warning, diver down, somebody get me a doctor. It was the best of both worlds, and we were sitting on top of the world, is that the ice cream man? Good enough, either that or poundcake. Oh, to get away and be unchained. 5150, always one more 5115.

Knowing I have him now. Making the videos to play back and hear him say he just wants to hear my voice. Talking to the TV I'm on. Was this tonight? You look like you're frozen. Oh, there it goes. How do I turn it off? You're here now, I don't need to watch you on the TV. You're here.

Somebody check on Shane Hawkins. Taylor's gone. Where's the memory?

My Hero. Dammit. Did it again.

Sacred Silence

Mellow the end, numb on the fringe
Calm peanut butter center
Disorder in order

The blank stare reminds of what you give
Who is the one on your mind?
Triumph today
Feels like we're running out of time
Don't get discouraged
Better to give than receive
Sitting in the sun
Laughing in the rain
Lead me on
Follow me down the road
Will you find who you are?
Now we have reason
Pass the evening with a drink and a friend
We let our skin get too thin

Sunny-Day Sleep

I love to sleep
To go on that adventure of the subconscious
Artistic temperament
It's an honest debate
Good night noon

Truth-Seeking Missile

Lots of love
Finding the way
To the center of your soul
And your authenticity

Game of Life

Hemingway
Williams
Even Thoreau

Hetfeild
Pinnick
Even Hagar

Bukowski
Vonnegut
Even Carver

Dylan
Simon
Even Wolfgang

Escher
Rockwell
Even Kincaid

Cameron
Martin
Even Cleese

Frost
Cummings
And even Angelou

Crichton
Atwood
And of course King

O'Keefe
Ross
and happy mistakes

This is the resume
Of a man bent on influence
Of words and musings of creative
I let them in
I let them dance
I asked them if this was a trance
To imagine
To wonder
To pretend on the lark
Every time I got lost
They led me from dark

Thank you, skills and talent
All those who've been there
You've made me dig deeper
And made me aware